Dr. Mike McManus has written a series of essays from July through December, 2009 for an audience of business degree students and the general public. These originally appeared on the blog site of the California International Business University (www.cibu.edu), and generated interest from people around the world. Three themes emerged: the crashing global economy and the new paradigm of investment chaos; ultimate human issues in being a global business "million mile flyer"; and the deep search for personal identity and purpose that is embedded in the careers of students and graduates. This short book is dedicated to the students and readers who care enough about these issues to want to do something... also to friends and future friends.

Contents

One

Introduction

Many years ago, I read and was impressed with Richard Selzer's now famous book *Letters to a Young Doctor*. Dr. Selzer M.D. wrote the book to inspire his students... hundreds of young medical doctors and surgeons who would go out to the world and heal the sick, perform surgery on the hopeful and hopeless cases, and dedicate their lives to the creed of higher values. Selzer was a teaching doctor at Yale Medical School. He based the book on a similar title by Rilke, *Letters to a Young Poet*. They were meant to inspire, teach and celebrate the collegiality of the profession in its greatest moments of triumph and its deepest moments of loss.

What occurs to me is that we too are training young professionals to assume positions which hold *life and death* in their grasp, the next generation of presidents of companies... some large and famous, some cozy and family in nature, and some will go out and create brand new organizations... **new to the world... ones that do not exist now.**

This past year I have chosen to speak out on several topics which are central to the lives of our students... the young presidents of the future. These are three messages which I choose to share at this stage of my thinking and art.

1. *Business schools must speak out on the new chaos factors in the global economic breakdown... we who manage them must articulate the role they have played in this stage of our planetary economy... and there has been a role, while not the worst of reasons and factors, it is in there and part of the ugliness. Young presidents must get this and be*

willing to act and speak out.

2. *Being part of a truly global community... understanding that you will be a million mile flyer, that you will go into and out of and through cultures and must navigate the geography and the human issues that come as everyday extraordinary moments, unexpected, and you must react... humanly and humanely as a leader, as the father-mother lion of the pride, ever vigilant, faster than any other, modest yet like a champion... you must be able to celebrate triumph, and handle tragedy. You set the pace. You must recognize its signals.*

3. *Someday, you must be willing to state your personal mission and commitment. This sounds easy. It is not. It is your personal statement as a scientist, creator, artist. Your relief is that great examples are out there. But you will first need to identify your mission and what is the central project or vision of your life... your energy and your articulation will follow. Then, there will be mysteries you cannot understand. Your heart may see what your mind cannot even begin to understand...*

So, young presidents, go forward. Your destiny may not be your choice. It may already be written in the stars. I share with you some of my own insights along my journey so far in these essays, some of my passions and concerns, some of my loved things in life and some of my great unknowns as well. Welcome to the young presidents society of the world. Your destiny is to lead and create good things, to help and heal the weak, to help the strong be better, build better engines and to enjoy your pride... it is after all your family that will see it all unfold first, before anyone else. You are in friendly company.

December, 2009

You are in and have come from a business school. So, what do you have to say about that, President _____?

Two

You and Wall Street... You and Main Street

President's Message

19 March 2009

B-Schools' Role in This Crisis?
A Case of Collective Responsibility... ?

Well, here we are again. Smack in the middle of a seemingly endless spiral of corporate failures, abuses, and huge economic losses that span the globe. Before jumping to simplistic conclusions, can we all agree that there is enough blame to go around? We may go through another Bretton Woods system, or a complete trashing of the new Mark to Market (M to M) accounting system. There will be some hard adjustments as the financial world searches for some new platform of global financial asset valuation and stability. It cannot be what today's market's last sale (M to M) will be... that just cannot prevail.

The role of business schools in where we have come from? Some would deny any role that b-schools have played into this mess. Let's be honest, folks, there has been a role, and here is what it has been... in the best East Coast USA b-schools, where this all started, for decades, finance professors have taught wealth creation go-go. The method has been to show their brilliance and superior qualities by creating financial vehicles in the laboratories of financial engineering. Fissile material for Main Street. Short selling, high-leverage speculation, CDO bundling of real estate assets, M to M accounting, derivatives, and of all things, the "synthetic bond market". This is all new stuff since I was in b-school in the sixties. And I was in a very good one. Yet everything, or nearly everything that has been done is "within the laws" of the United States and its states within.

At the risk of mentioning the unmentionable... the doctrine of "collective responsibility", defined by Wikipedia as a belief that individuals may be held responsible for others' actions by tolerating, ignoring, or harboring them without active collaboration. This doctrine is very powerful and invokes emotion... it is after all what governments use at a time of war to define the battlefield. So now, faculty members from several large and very, very prestigious business schools have shared the deep concern that they now are being queried and pursued in non-friendly ways about their role in the business school establishment and the link to the Wall Street collapse. "Our professional legacy is on the line", exclaimed a faculty friend from one of America's top five b- schools! Many of us as individual professional academics decry and deny this link as it concerns our own personal professional activities. Most of us have had nothing to do at all with the criminal element or the irrationally exuberant finance professors who created the monsters. But, did any of us publicly disassociate ourselves or disclaim our institutions? Likely not, we fit the definition of collective responsibility as a culture of business school leaders and leading academics. The most culpable are the very leaders from the b-schools that are the laboratories for Wall Street itself. The producers of the fissile materials.

So, where does the deepest and most corrupt value lie? Now watch this. We all teach and the world all accept that we must learn to outsmart our competitors. That is what competitive intelligence is all about... intuition and tenacity. But some faculty have, in their attempt to show brilliance and vigor, gone the next seemingly logical step in their teaching and influence... outsmart the customer and now outsmart the investor. What seems like straight line logic has become the middle level Wall Street breeder ground for a complete historical financial shakedown and huge backlash.

B-schools are not at all completely nor even hugely to blame, but for prominent professors and Deans and b-school leaders to deny any connection is wrong. It would be like allowing nuclear scientists to create fissile new substances in a laboratory with no concern for the use and care or oversight of the impact of their work. When the managers of those labs are responsible, they will not deny their reality.

To impose creeds or signed moral oaths to b-students to be "good citizens" is shallow. The best and worst criminals would so sign! It is also a false promise to hang our emphasis on the new paradigm of "green" or "CSR" or "sustainable economy leaders"... that would be to turn b-schools into public policy institutes of political correctness. To give up the teaching of b-ethics is not a solution, though all the Wall Street crooks came through those classes too. So what's up, doc, for the Dean or b-school leader to do?

We acknowledge we are producing people (our graduates) for the world of business. We cannot deny or minimize the importance of our finance laboratories and the messaging (particularly the wealth creation for "me" theme) that faculty are using to shape the next generation of entrants to business. There is absolutely no b-school cure, no "off the hook" excuse. We have a responsibility to have active, open, intellectual debate and discussion of these issues, in our classrooms, in our hallways, on our whiteboards, on our blogs.

I think it is something about challenging the false logic that outsmarting the competitor means it is also OK to outsmart the investor. So what have the ivory tower finance wizards and their Wall Street prodigy proven in these decades of their "brilliance" and cleverness? Were they trying to vie with lawyers for the smartest kids in town label? If so, and maybe, then it has brought us all down several notches compared to where we could have been. As the renowned astrophysicist, Jeffrey Bennett, has observed, our civilization's accumulation of knowledge has far outpaced our civilization's ability to apply that knowledge in beneficial ways for us and our children. If that can be the central challenge of an astronomer, why can it not be our challenge in the business world too? Financial laboratories are dealing with fissile material. Financial laboratories exist in b-schools. We (b-schools) produce people for the world of business. Do I need say anything more?

The challenge of this education is immense. It is absolutely not centered in a show of brilliance or extreme cleverness or institutional ego. It also must provide practical education for the hard working, non-spoiled, average students, who need summer job, part time work, engagement to get their education paid for. I worked in steel mills summers and waited tables in the Ivy League to help get through. I was a graduate assistant to the max every semester of my graduate education. This all brought huge rewards. You don't have to have as "gritty" an experience as I did, but consider the central role of hard work, and what non-Wall Street thinking possibilities may be for b-students... it gives some fresh horizons and whole new meaning to the idea of a b-school! We are also here to help our students create their dream and career concept for the long distant future if we can. This will almost inevitably bring us back to our central role in creating greater wealth through creating leadership seekers and entrepreneurs... wealth is not the strategy, but rather the outcome. The strategy is to create real and new things, to build the skills and awareness to do so, and to be a laboratory for that, not a breeding ground for faculty and students to go out and spread the financial fissile material that may fall into the wrong hands...

The Legacy

19 April 2009

1. **YOUR STUDENTS** What are you telling your Finance Majors right now? What are you telling them about employability? What are you doing to help your unemployed Alums?

2. **YOUR FACULTY** Which of your faculty members confuse "outsmart the competitor" with "outsmart the customer/investor"?

3. **YOU AS LEADER** Have you as an educational leader spoken out publicly about extremes in corporate greed?

4. **YOUR INSTITUTIONAL VALUES** Do any members of your faculty articulately urge excesses in extreme financial self interest, egotism, and hubris?

5. **YOUR TUITION POLICY** What have been your Business School's annual tuition increases over the last five years and how do you explain these increases?

6. **YOUR CONSISTENCY** If you advocate students signing oaths or pledges, how do you intend to make these enforceable?

7. **YOUR CREDIBILITY** Would you be willing to revoke the degrees or discredit any of your alums who become convicted white collar felons?

8. **YOUR PUBLIC RESPONSIBILITY** Are you willing to engage in a public forum discussion and debate on these issues? Will you offer your stage as a place for this debate on a national scale?

9. **YOUR INNOVATION** What, if anything, can you offer as any new approach or pedagogy to the teaching of ethics in your MBA curriculum?

10. **YOUR INTEGRITY** Are you willing to publicly disclose the names and detailed sources of significant grants or gifts to your institution?

President Obama and Business Schools...

06 May 2009

The FASB (Federal Accounting Standards Board) relaxed rules last month and the rigid M to M (Mark to Market) rules for real estate and asset valuation that banks must use in determining and reporting their reserve and loan ratios are now more in favor of lending. BUT, many big banks still carry what the industry has called "level 2" assets... those which the rules say still must use "fire-sale" values instead of historical, standardized values. This means that we are far from seeing the end of the banking crisis and there will be a longer period of winter than hoped for.

Take Two. In evaluating faculty for tenure, publications are the heavy standard for determining who gets lifetime employment and who must go. Believe it or not, academia has evolved now an increasingly accepted POINT SYSTEM for evaluating a faculty member's publications... right down to arbitrary go-no-go points for certain journals and media. We have seen the increasing use of QUANTITATIVE MODELS for measuring essentially QUALITATIVE phenomena. Whether bankers telling you your house is worth yesterday's sale price (M to M) or your being told "bye bye" because your publications just don't have the point weight that meets the cut off for tenure... you are being measured by mathematical models! What is your FICO lately? How's your self worth, by the way?

This will not end, and our President even asked last weekend, "Do we need more engineers, or do we need more engineers going to Wall Street to become derivative traders?"The role of B-schools is NOT to produce derivative traders (a few maybe), but business creators who go out and manage qualitative things without needing quantitative models to make the big decision.

The role of B-school leaders is to point this out. How's your FICO? How is your "level 2" asset portfolio doing? What is your Rolex worth? What are you worth? Roll the credits, please, for the qualitative model builders, the business creators, the champions of the economy. Not the ivory tower cubicle geniuses.

Merrill Lynch or Meryl Streep?

14 May 2009

This article is a royal example of the magical tricks that Wall Street wizards and B-school math-drenched MBA's may just be playing (don't forget some lawyers as well) on most of the rest of us. Get ready for another dip in bank portfolios. M to M philosophy has not been reigned in. It still drives the value of what you own and what you rent. If you are a renter, the market chaos may be in your favor. If you own and have invested, you are hiding.

We had many of our recent MBA graduates dream of secure MBA-style world class jobs at Merrill Lynch or Private Wealth Management, _____ Bank. Gone. Whew! Where are these good people morphing to for employment? We are starting see the stars align in some sectors where "digital convergence" is taking root... like Hollywood/Media/Business/Entertainment sector... media marketing was, after all, our recent cutting edge MBA elective course. Forget Merrill Lynch. Get a job with Merrill Streep as her media business consultant. She has outlasted and will Merrill Lynch. SN (Social Networking, not Saturday Night) is the enlarging ingredient. The "yeast" of the new edge.

As CIBU approaches another graduation, we reflect on our purpose and how we can give lasting value to our students. It is not going to come by following old horses. Light up the night and look for the comets out there!

The Tarp Is Off, The Sack Is ON

29 July 2009

In blogs, we have fun, we poke fun, and we poke seriously at issues. I have been writing and blogging lately about M to M (Mark to Market) accounting, and am convinced that it is the root of the global financial problem and fixing it is the root of our way out. Blogs are also for poetry and operas in words... so here we go one more time. My concern as you read my poetry is that you understand that B-schools have a role... in the problem, and now, more importantly, in the solution...

The average Goldman Sachs employee (23,000 worldwide) just made $770,000 pay bonus up through third quarter 2009. Their TARP is paid off. They declared this bonus in public in mid July,2009. The average homeowner in the US lost much in 2009 to the downward spiral of Mark to Market (MtoM) accounting rules and thinking. The five Connecticut FASB gurus softened it in April, but the fall is still killing values all over the place. Few SEC busts. Lots of "personal wealth" made lately by a few, while the vast majority watch and suffer in confusion and fuzzy logic. Go Green, get the Hybrid. If the walls could talk, what fortunes are made on the inside. Why is no one listening? The ghost of Watergate is busted. The teaching goes on. New York, New York! Make your fortune on short sell... derivatives is the new "plastics" in the Graduate. Dustin would remember. And Meryl Streep outlived Merrill Lynch. Get to Wall Street, my son, my daughter, before it is too late. Before Bernie's "feeders and machers" rout you out. The heat is on. The bonuses roll. The values plummet. OK enough innuendo and poetry. M to M thinking, rules, benefactors - that is our problem. Professors in the Finance Departments, your cleverness is challenged to reinvent a gentler and kinder set of modified, hybrid M to M rules to match the global and US need for a stable platform. If you don't do this soon your name may come up when the feeders snitch and the masses wake up. You can now "outsmart" your mentors and reinvent some fancy models that save the system, and the life savings of your fellow countrymen and women. You can prove how smart you are, if you are indeed smart. The listeners are coming. Your role could be the savior of the economic system as we know it. Get M to M fixed and restore sanity and reasonableness to us all. Your chaotic models and teachings have benefited the few, not the greater good. Your "cleverness" was wasted on our national trustthe best and bright who attended your classes and learned the models and hatched with you the angles that shifted money from Detroit families to special addresses you know. Professors in the Wall Street Ivy Tower, listen up... it is a mean message I hear rolling in from Main Street. They are coming for you. Your only chance is humility, not cleverness. The only way is to disassemble M to M. Build it back, pay forward, Professors of the Wall Street Ivy Tower. Satan is proud of your extreme cleverness. Did you ever in your farthest thoughts, think of the virtues of the average guy? It is not too late.

Is Anybody Out there listening:
If So, Here's How to Prove it...

01 September 2009

In recent weeks, I have chronicled what I believe is the prime root of the current economic global crisis... the ever advancing of the M to M (Mark to Market) accounting standards ethic of valuing real assets at their lowest possible scavenger market value. I have also advanced a theory as to how the true Wall Street scavengers (short sellers and their greater constituency) have benefited while middle America has been injured. My position is supported in concept by Nobel laureate Paul Krugman of Princeton University.

Yet, nothing is really happening. Let me list several pieces of my evidence to support this hypothesis that we are not only seeing the 'greening' of America, but also the sleeping sickness of the middle class as to what has been really going on.

1. The FDIC backup reserves have plummeted. The fund covers 0.22 percent of insured deposits. The FDIC will not release the list of the truly problematic banks. Washington.

2. The number of problem financial institutions is up 36% (second quarter, 2009). Washington.

3. The FASB has not made a major policy move on M to M rules (essentially allowing the predators to rule accounting valuations) since April, 2009. Connecticut.

4. I found a really interesting article in my literature chest... "How Bad Management Hides Behind Self-Protection", co authored

by Thomas Friedman, in the Florida Trend periodical, dated, March 1983... "selling out has become a controversial tool for management trying to exercise self interest"...

5. Thomas Friedman today writes to try to explicate the complexity of the global economy and how we can see our way through a flatter world. He has been doing so since 1983!

6. Michael Milken was indicted on over 80 separate counts of securities fraud for being the king of "junk bonds", and for being involved in inside trading affairs. All is forgiven. He is a free agent today. California.

7. Ivan Boesky was the icon of insider trading in the 1980's... all is forgiven.

8. The deals of today involve computers which have the speed of light as a competitive advantage in placing competitive bids on the big electronic trading board. New York.

9. Who controls this all? Washington or New York? (I say New York)

10. Are there insiders operating today? New York.

11. If so, why have we not heard of this? New York.

12. How could the SEC have so long turned a blind eye to Bernie Madoff and his operations and the team behind him? Washington and New York (working together)

13. Is it possible that there are highly integrated finance and tech teams operating in super stealth mode on select stocks to benefit a select few? New York.

14. Why has Congress not properly exercised its oversight functions on these issues to allow the oversight to fall to a highly politicized press where no one has any final authority? Washington.

I am a Wall Street observer and have Bachelors in Economics from the Wharton School, and have built up a business school for students from around the world to come to America and study our best and brightest ideas and people. I do have something to say here. I do read and follow the issues and have researched the deeper issues within the daily press issues.

So, if Tom Friedman cannot be really heard since his earlier calls of 1983, if Paul Krugman is really not being listened to by Wall Street, if insiders are seemingly free to roam... where are we?

We are no further than our noses in terms of what we thought we learned in the 80's, the 90's, and until now.

If you understand these concerns and feel you wish to express your opinion, let our blog be your forum...

Let's see what a grass roots effort might look like...

I will keep you posted on the major signs of real change.

For now it is onward with insider trading, SEC back-seat travel, bold cheaters, business schools which champion the wrong heroes, and people like me who still think that if Ben Franklin were alive today, he would not lose faith in our system... but he would be thinking of inventing something that we have not seen yet which may fix the basic problem. What is that? More to come...

You deal with human cultures and peoples of such difference every day. What do you do to contribute to that greater community?

Three

On Becoming a Global Citizen

Going Down Under:
Another Turn of Psychological Geography

23 July 2009

I have always been amused with how we humans view and understand our space, distance, scale and how it fits us on our planet. Especially how we view where we are, where we are willing and wanting to travel and whether it is psychologically near or far whatever the actual distance. Just a very recent example to share in my own life... Until several months ago, I had rarely even allowed the thought of going all the way down under, as they say, to Australia. For many of us from North America, even California, the center of my own personal universe, it always seemed so very far away. Just 21 million people living on Earth's largest and driest island, the size of the US. The geographical size of New Jersey, Taiwan has a larger population! Australia had mystique, distance, boldness, vastness to it. That made it seem farther somehow. Here we go again, I said with psychological geography, I define, as that distance and scale and space which we define not by hours of plane travel, actual miles, effort, or effortless, but purely as a subjective thing in our mind. My wife was our urging to go. We needed a getaway. We had the miles in our United points. The flights and even hotels would cost next to nothing. It is winter in Sydney, but it all came together. We would have five days there and 2.5 days in the air. A glorious week to the farthest place on the globe! We are going. Decision made. We are going to the farthest place I know. As the days approached before takeoff, it seemed like I was entering a realm of disbelief in what we had just engineered! What if... how could we manage at that distance? The dogs at home alone... the school... all the reasons why this made no sense. It was so far. But mostly in my mind. Welcome to the planet of psychological geography! Guess what? The flight time from Vancouver (Yes, we were routed there as a departure gateway by Air Canada) was a bare 16.5 hours... mind you, just 1.5 hours more than last year's flight from SFO to Hong Kong. I've been to China 15 times, and Taiwan over 30, and those flights are just 2 hours less than to Australia... into winter we go. Take of roll was long. Lots of fuel and a full 777 loaded for AUS. In 30 minutes, we were at initial cruising altitude 33,000 feet, 550 mph, tailwind, with 7700 overwater miles to go into a 14 hour night of blackness. But, what sweet places we would fly over... just south of the Big Island, Fiji, Howland Island, New Caledonia, then landfall at sunrise into approach control Sydney for an earlier than scheduled landing at 815 am. What a sweet touchdown here on this runway at Sydney International. We are in Australia, the place I always wondered if I would ever see.

As we fly so normally so often to Europe from California, and to mid Asia, we take for granted these long distances. They become in our minds just another work milk run. We were so adrenaline high from just the thought of where we were it was impossible to be tired, so we walked the city of Sydney and enjoyed its Chinatown to the max, just like anywhere. At night, I was not even tired. We were after all sitting on floor 26, looking down at the lights of this magnificent jewel of a city, an Olympic City, just as you might imagine it to be. Not like Mars, or Antarctica, but just like a place you have always been, just like it is everywhere else. But we were in Australia!!! "Australia" came from a Dutch word meaning "lower lands and territories"... they drive on the wrong side of the road, but water still flows downhill and dogs bite. Pandas do not. Five marvelous days went by. The most incredible moments were the beaches, with powerful surf, the warmth of the people, and the tameness of the Panda we touched and were photographed with. The warmth of the people, the warmth of the people. Yes, that was Australia.

Back in my office in a week, 7 time zones, 12.5 hours SYD to SFO, our dogs are fine, plants still growing, lawn green, all is well... no fatigue, no jet lag. Whew, I really want to go back. So, we learn, and we learn again where is home and how far we may go to understand ourselves in this space we live in, and how (now this is the really essential thing) we may put up these strange barriers all our life about how far away someplace is, until we actually go there and then it is part of our travel-able world, it is never far away again, and we will go back. We will go back. We will go back. Thank you Air Canada, and again United for so well showing us what you can do with machines and navigation. We appreciate how frail we are... speeding along at 550 mph over 7700 miles of night water... how rarely, if ever, anything goes wrong. Thank you again. Australia, you just did your so natural thing and won some new friends who want to come back. Friends, share with me your thoughts about how far you think things are and how your mind has shaped your geography. A sense of place is home. A sense of distance is only what we make it to be. You can go to Australia in your lifetime... it is very worth doing, and now is no better time! It is not so far away, after all.

In our world of global business education, this is one of the biggest of lessons.

Return to Psychological Geography: Part Two

18 August 2009

In an earlier piece about our recent trip to Australia, I marveled about the scale of distances and how we went to that great place so far away the I hardly thought I would ever go, until we did go, had five great days there and were back in a week at the same office, same desk, same stuff. Eighteen thousand miles. Fourteen thousand night miles over water. Koalas, "Mate" and all. Blink, you're there, blink, you're back. Still, after all the travel I've done, I say Wow!

Psychological Geography, I defined as the distances we have in our mind, and how we think about those distances, far or near. With incredible jet travel, it can be far or near, and may not actually relate to the "real distances". I wonder if pilots have this? I know I do... wake up in a hotel, look at the ceiling and for a split second, say, "where am I?... Oh, yes, it is Germany, or Paris, or Taipei, or Pittsburgh, or Sydney..."

Two friends who are both outspoken and intellectual in their nature have told me that this concept is interesting to them. I think it is so with many.

But, why?

What does this say about our inner world? Not the one of check-in counters, baggage limits, mileage charts, air traffic control... the world of our mind. The world is flat to many... one big global village. If India burns lots of carbon, Los Angeles feels it weeks later. Teens around the globe all rock to the same sounds and jump on Facebook. Small village. Most will never get on airplanes and travel across oceans, actually. Many will do it in their mind. That is good enough for some.

We measure our inner world by what we know and feel and what is possible. There is no scale to it. No consistent measuring stick. We travel time and place and dream.

On some rare occurrences, some get the chance to do actual distance travel. In the scale of thousands of miles over dark oceans, actual oceans with big fish and unnavigable waves below.

One of our human gifts is our inner sense of geography. We can appreciate real distance more. We may never actually come to grips with how much we travel and how fast and how frail the journey. One mistake and we may be lost. But most of us make it.

We in the global business world need to appreciate distance more. We have a dual world of actual geography and the geography of what we imagine, what we may dream and what we may stretch to believe that we may visit someday.

I am still amazed with our visit to Australia. It is actually far away, yet so near. It is so within reach. The Koalas are really worth spending some time with. Sydney is worth seeing in real terms.

My two friends are two of the most educated and worldly wise people I know. One is even very mystical. He knows of the Hawaiian spirit of Pele (the goddess of spirit-fire) first hand. He has seen the white dog and the old woman with white hair, the spirits of Pele. He knows *psychological geography*. I had no explaining to do. It was for him like seeing the spirit of Pele again, just another form.

Alas, I connected my friend to the dimension with me of time-space in mind. He travelled there before. Pele visited after all.

The world of global business will log you a million actual miles. Get ready. Your heart may take you to places your mind cannot begin to understand.

Philosophy at Thirty-Thousand Feet

19 August 2009

Some of us in higher education have a Ph. D. Many do not realize that that actually means a *"doctor of philosophy"*. Philosophy means the love of wisdom. Wisdom comes from the knowledge of the ages.

A friend recently shared with me his suggestion that more of us in business education need to write philosophy, that it may be a more effective bridge between leaders than most other topics.

Consider how important someone feels when they are asked for their wisdom! Their accumulated knowledge and how they see the world. There are few things that are as great a compliment.

I have gravitated in that direction in my writing, and it seems productive. To wit my recent thoughts on what I have called *psychological geography*. Most of us who fly thousands of miles over water and lands and cultures to get to planned business meetings have little appreciation for the geography, actual and perceived that we traverse. The cultures we fly over, the nature we never see because we are going too fast and too high. We grab the minutes and hours we can and take our digital cameras and get what we can between meetings. We see the cultures from taxicab windows. We are ushered around and design elaborate schemes for our students to travel and study other cultures like we did when we were young, but, we are moving too fast as leaders to see up close and personal what we want our students to see.

I once sat on United flights to Europe and Asia exactly beside the same executive from Silicon Valley, purely by chance. He and I were amazed. It actually got me thinking that maybe the frequent flyer program has a secret code to place former travelers together again, when they can! What a benefit! What if we could actually tell them what we would like for a flight neighbor, actually fill out a questionnaire and let them match us all up!

Ah, if we could slow down and smell the roses, if only we could stop briefly and enjoy the cultures we assume we know and travel so fast through on our way to meetings.

When I reflect on the best conversations I have had while on these long flights, it is about philosophy. It always gets around to that somehow. The collective business wisdom of the ages. A bridge. A safe place to explore. A welcome ground. The love of wisdom, after all!

Four

Who Are You?

An Institutional Mission Commitment, One Person at a Time

19 August 2009

Our CIBU Mission Statement encapsulates a terse commitment to provide a valuable educational and professional preparation for the global business economy. We do our best to state our purpose in a few, concise words, politically-correct, timely, universal, and personal.

Lately, I have been writing on the theme of bringing a relevant personal dialog to globalism, and a sense of professional and personal psychology to the global business world.

We are in the business of bringing this message with clarity and zeal to each person in our educational community, every student in our classes, and many in or readership *one person at a time*.

CIBU is somewhat different. It is intimate, family, community, intense, focused. It has students from many highly different cultures and politics. All aspire to the degrees that are now globally universal and fairly similar (more similar than different) across most universities... the bachelor's the master's and the doctoral degrees. So what's the quintessential ingredient that makes us different?

We differ from the basic premise of *mass market higher education*. We do not strive for economies of scale. We do strive for qualities of scale - small scale - we master the advantages of scale. We are not dependent on public support or funding... there are no public service mandates on us. We champion the individual, not the collective. We specialize in global teams, not cultural dominance of one style over all.

We are an American institution. We inherit the intellectual heritage of Ben Franklin, Henry Thoreau, the modest style of Abe Lincoln, the bravery of Eleanor Roosevelt and Amelia Earhart and the mental acuity of Bill Gates and Steve Jobs. We embrace the cause of the yet-to-be-born entrepreneur hero. We will have graduates who build companies and some who build family and societal systems with integrity. We will have some who need others just to stand up. We hope we can be there to help.

Thus, the CIBU quality is one of utmost personal education. You cannot get lost in our system. You may choose to be shy, but you will have your chance to shine and be your own hero. And if you are a star, or if you want to be a star, this university will find you.

We are intensely committed to your personal journey with us. We are committed to preparing you to fly a million miles and be a global business star. We will teach you the points of the journey, the markers that we all have seen, but we want to show you how to deeply see and appreciate all the cultures and systems you will fly over at incredible heights and at incredible speeds. You will have lifetime memories that begin here. There are some that we cannot begin to understand until you begin the journey with us. They are bigger than anything you can now imagine. So, get ready, join us here at CIBU for an educational foundation for your career and the makings of the magic and miracles that only being here can bring. It will be among the best years of your life, day by day, one person at a time.

Creating Lifetime Memories:
A Daily Passion that Does Not Happen Every Day

20 August 2009

I get to write about this subject. It took me a while. I needed to get ready. There is fierce awesomeness in this topic, not like others I have written before. There is respectful fear and trepidation, the kind that comes from knowing you were caught up in maybe a sacred moment.

If I do my job as President of CIBU, I seek moments in which the ordinary becomes extraordinary. I have the chance, not every day, not even often, but once in a splendid while to help something along to become a huge moment of importance and greatness for someone in our community of CIBU. Some thread, which if pulled, unravels into a lifetime memory.

So, as this story goes (and it is a true story), this student from France this year was going to run in the San Diego Rock and Roll Marathon. I heard this second hand from another student, let's say the messenger. It seemed quite "cool" at that moment, when I heard it, that this runner was also a firefighter by training. A long distance runner and a firefighter. None of these things are by accident, rather by choice. Quite impressive, I thought several days before the actual marathon.

Maybe by chance, I read an article in the local news about a war widow, a young American woman, who lost her husband in the ravages of the Iraq war... a woman who planned to run her second marathon in loving memory of her husband. Last year she did also and had a hard time getting through part of the course that ran through the Marine base downtown. She planned to run this marathon for her husband. It was her second marathon for him.

The article seared something deep, something powerful in my soul and I knew this had a connection. I was supposed to see this. I could have missed it so easily.

I saw our CIBU student the day before the race. The student who was the messenger brought her by. I showed her the article and she read it top to bottom. I went to my front office and grabbed a small American flag. I gave it to her and asked if she might run with it in the marathon in memory of this woman. She smiled and said she would do it and she would find her. I told her it might be hard... there were to be 20,000 people in that race... I left it alone.

The race came and went. But the next week, the student who was the messenger came and said that there was something that happened that they wanted to share with me. They came into my office. OK, I said, did you see her? No, not at the race... she waited several hours at the finish line after running a 3:39 marathon, but this firefighter did not find the American widow. She wanted to give her the flag.

Messengers play special roles in these dramas. This one figured out a way to find this American marathon runner... where she worked... through Facebook! They went to meet her. The meeting took place, the flag was given to her as a gift and a memory by our student. A picture was taken of the two of them with the small American flag. That picture will be in my office as long as I am there and the memory will be with them for a long, long time. But it was somehow not finished. Our student did her job, that no one ever gave her to do. I had one more small American flag. I gave it to her as her gift of our friendship. France and America, after all, have learned to stick together for hundreds of years of our countries' histories. The messenger's picture was not with these two. She said it was not important. She was just the driver, that's all, she said. The story will go on.

In our lives, we sometimes see the chance to make a difference and do something that creates a lifetime memory for someone. We take the chance and make it happen. These moments are sealed and can never be undone. They are the moments of circumstance, yet we somehow can recognize them and act, as messengers, as drivers, as players in the life dramas that stay real and vivid forever.

Presidents can sometimes find these moments. Professors and teachers find them often. Fellow students and friends find them... we all find them. The choice is to act, to not mind being bold and brave and doing something incredible.

I tell this story with such respect for the American friend, whom I shall probably never meet, but for whom my heart goes out. I hope she felt the friendship of two of our CIBU students from France who came to love America, San Diego and every moment here.

These are the great moments of CIBU community. There are so many untold stories of the new friends made here through our doors and out in our California air and sun. This is the essence of our university. And it all happens by chance. Marvelous, exquisite, many-splendored, beautiful chance.

Just so you know, this was not... my average day...

The Story Will Go On:
Messengers Cannot Appear at Center Stage

27 August 2009

In the last story, we chronicled how a student we called a "messenger" played a pivotal role in helping a miraculous thing to happen. A French Marathon student running in San Diego met and gave an

American flag to an American heroine running in the same race - a symbol of respect, friendship and love for America and San Diego.

The messenger was the driver. She accompanied the runner when she finally met her friend the other runner. Flags were given as gifts. One to the American heroine, and another to the French runner, our CIBU student, who ran a great 3:39 marathon race with deep purpose.

One last flag remained as my gift to the messenger, my way of saying thanks for keeping this whole thing on track, for sensing the potential of the event, who was happy just to have helped, not to be a player herself. I had the small American flag as my farewell gift to this third person in this three-person drama. The other two flags were also gifts born of inspiration.

But sometimes our lives just don't slow down fast enough for us to complete the most important of small things.

I saved the flag for our farewell meeting as best we had planned to see each other before this student flew back to France to resume her normal life in her home country. For logistical reasons, the farewell meeting did not happen and I still have the flag, and it will be hers when I see her next. In France. Appropriate. As we said earlier, France and America have learned to stick together for nearly 300 years, why should it change now?

These are such small things and we move so fast through life before we even know what may have happened. We just act and hope for the best.

I should have known, and given the gift earlier. Messengers never show up for the glory. They perform their acts of heroism and leave as quickly as they arrive. They do not like center stage. Don't ask them to be a star. They will be in the background making sure others are stars.

There was no lost time, there was only a great story and some great actions that made lifetime memories. As we say "a bien tot" to some of our students, we say "bienvenue" to the new ones. There will be new dramas. They will have deep meaning and emotion. They will not ever touch the power of this story, but they will have new power unto each of the individuals who experience them. For some students, it is so difficult and painful to leave San Diego, and so sweet to land in home country where home is so close. For us too, this separation process is also a natural and healthy process. It makes the days unusual. It keeps the circle complete. It reminds some of us that distances are both real and psychological.

28

We will complete the flag circle, and keep the torch passed to the next visitors to this place on the planet, meanwhile realizing our place in the greater scheme of things. We are trying to be rational players in a wildly chaotic planetary economy. When we are lucky, we slow things down enough to bring about strokes of boldness and bravery. As we all fly a million miles to mostly planned events and meetings on the planet, maybe we can be aware of what is actually happening all around us, most of the time.

Friendship is the Name, 911 is Here Again

11 September 2009

Just over a year ago, CIBU honored United Captain Mark Hoog and his best friend, United Captain Jason Dahl, the pilot lost in United 93 on September 11, 2001. We honored them for their service, and not least for the friendship they had. They received our highest honor, the honorary doctorate... one very much alive and working and producing as a creative professional, ... and one very much gone from us, but a national hero and someone still here strong in spirit, as close as you allow yourself to see, feel, touch his spirit. Friendship. The "ship of friends"... something rare... something quite precious when it happens between and among colleagues who work together, whether in offices, or on airships that move an incredible heights and speeds and help to glue together our global world. Its 251 am, late, can't sleep, just woke after a dream about friendship I too have had with colleagues in my workplace. So, back to the keyboard once again, to share this 9-11-09 thought with you.

What makes it happen, I don't know. I suppose I never will, though the theory of random events may just explain it. I mean, you put yourself in the workplace with hundreds of people over time, and someone, sometime, somewhere is going to just have that immeasurable chemistry with you and you with him or her, right? Just random in the population, say out of 100 workmates, maybe at least 20 or 30 who will be "friends", right? Maybe out of the 20 or 30, there will be five or three or one who are lifetime friends. That is not so hard to understand.

Captain Mark and Captain Jason were thrown together by United flight training program for senior Captains. Mark dedicated many of his creative acts to Jason his friend, lost in duty. They are still on the "ship of friends"

In CIBU's business, we see a big flock of graduates enjoy the commencement ceremony and we all say "hello" and "a bien tot", till next time, sometimes "goodbye" after the ceremony. Often, we think we will see them again. Rarely is that ever true. Oh, don't misunderstand me, some wander back in and we have wonderful reunions and see each other again. It is really fun when that happens. Watching them grow. Seeing the progress that only work experience can bring. We are then friends again, on the "ship of friends" again for a while.

Did you ever take a group trip or a group excursion? Really lots of bonding together, pictures, meals, laughter. It really builds friends. We remember these trips like they were yesterday.

This friendship thing is always interesting to me. It spans all kinds of borders and issues that should keep us apart, yet, miraculously, the ship of friends goes on, sails on... it is ageless. It cuts through age and time. I have true friends who are students younger than my own children, yet I think there is a timeless quality to the friendship and they have expressed it as well. Not too many, just a few who stay tuned and I see them over the years. About some, I feel like they are my children, or maybe brothers and sisters in some kind of celestial family that I cannot begin to understand. I just go with it. The Ship of Friends... I get on, they get on, we take a marvelous voyage together, get off and go on and on in our daily routine.

This date brings special meaning to many Americans... special emotion... the story of Mark Hoog and Jason Dahl and their friendship is how I am choosing to think of things this day, even as early in it as it is, now 320 am.

Cherish the times you see yourself on the Ship of Friends with someone. It is one for the snapshot album of your life. A true gift, ageless, priceless, when it happens. You can even see it happening all around most days... we are allowed this gift. On the most hallowed of days, with all its history, I choose to fly the Ship of Friends... so its boarding time now... I can't wait to see all those faces I love... we will all be on this journey again for a short but marvelous ride...

Sun will be up here in Pacific time zone in three hours, another September 11 morning... fresh coffee, sun, newspaper, almost time for another day at the office... sail on, Ship of Friends.

The Ship of Friends, "Friendship", ... What it Really Means?

29 September 2009

The blog piece I wrote on 9/11 at 3 am generated enormous and wonderful reactions from friends and students around the world. Some responses were from people I have not known who were moved by the idea of the "Ship of Friends". This outpouring has suggested that this "Ship" really exists, and is in all of our minds. Some have talked about the joy. Some have shared the pain of leaving friends. Getting on and off the ship...

- This is bigger than I ever thought it was.

- I will be responding in the days ahead...

- International students feel this deeply...

- Friends of internationals feel this deeply...

- More people need to feel this deeply...

- I will do my best to define what this "Ship of Friends" is...

- how it looks...

- when you know you have found it...

- what might be practical ways to make it work for you, i. e. internships. friendship families, "true friends" ...

- I guess, how to "join it"...

CIBU has humbly welcomed student-citizens from over 80 countries of the world. That is a true "ship of study". What it will take or it to be a true "Ship of Friends"... we will explore in the days ahead... this is a new frontier for myself to deeply, passionately explore in words and meaning for you what our ultimate Community is. There have been some very persuasive colleagues here lately who have advocated the idea of an energized global international business community around CIBU.

I know one thing. Friendships are the glue and the Ship of Friends concept is so very relevant to you and us...

More to come about this Ship!

Just another day at the office... oh, yes,... and have a nice coffee... and think about what a great opportunity you have with CIBU!

The Ship of Friendships: Explained (I Promised)

08 November 2009

One thing I know is that this Ship exists. Students and strangers from around the world have responded to my earlier blog on this topic... they know it... they have joined the ship and now are listening for more...
As a social scientist, I am expected to be 'empirical'... data based! That I can be. Now, it is my pleasure to share my intuition on top of the data... so here goes...

- It appears that the Ship is in our minds. It is not a virtual ship, though we may have fun visualizing a cruise ship or an airplane... we think of times we were on an actual voyage with ones we loved... The Ship is rather timeless... it does not have a need to define itself in terms of a special period of years or months or a specific part of a person's life... The passengers with us (our nearest and dearest) are ageless. This means that that whatever your age, your fellows may be older, younger, it does not matter so much... The passengers feel a very special bond. A kindred spirit. Something like family... brother-sisters, parent-child, or just comrades... ... but the bond is strong. Romance is not part of it as a central feature, though it can have some aspects. It is emotional. These things that put us on the same ship are strong... they are based on deep feelings, sharings and some kind of common experiences... This is important, this all cuts across cultures... it can happen in minutes, hours days, weeks, but it has little to do with where the people are born. If there are strong cultural differences, people on the Ship are able to short-cut these and deal very quickly with personal bonding...

- Music helps... see # 10-15

- Meeting with each other helps lots... how cannot we connect out hearts and minds if we do now share a near or some evening together once in a while

- Faith. If you do not know what this is , check with others... they can tell you...

- Your philosophy, your own... what you actually believe... are you truly open minded and do you have some pride in this? If not, danger signal... if so... celebrate with others...

- Environment... "really do miss your smile... there's a warm wind blowing the stars around and I'd really love to see you tonight... " (words from the unforgettable music of England Dan and John Ford Coley...... have you ever been in the desert, with a warm wind blowing and the stars are just THERE... Yes, the environment matters... it can be romantic, or compelling...

- I have been to paradise but I have never been to me. Georgia to California to ... anywhere I could run... (thanks Charlene) Truth is that is...

- Forever in my heart, even when I am gone, you will be here with me... forever (Thanks, Kenny Loggins)... ... ... I'll be yours... FOREVER

- When will I see you again? Wait forever? Hearts be together... in love or just friends... beginning or just the end... (thanks Three Degrees)

- Here you are again... thanks, Kelly Clarkson

- Its late September and I really think I should be back at school... (Rod Stewart) said it all.

The songs over our lives' years collect the themes of the Ship. The Ship has all these friends on it. With dearest and looking for dearest... and music...

The Ship is our boat in our minds. It is where we collect friends, music, friends, lovers, foes...

Some get on with us and some leave us...

It is what we have NOW.

What is it for CIBU?... It is what we all are... all our cultures, clicking instantly or separately... we try to hold respect for each others family, country, culture...

It is an ENVIRONMENT OF LEARNING in which we can listen and ask, "oh, tell me more"...

The SHIP OF FRIENDS is leaving port...

The Ship of Friends is us, folks, ... it is going somewhere... an international community slowly growing across nations with appreci-

ation, and a big message of welcome... to join the "SHIP OF FRIENDS"!
The Ship of Friends has destination, direction and momentum.

It is a lifelong challenge to join it or not.

What is a Full Life?

16 November 2009

Are we passive passengers or are we driving the ship? Does each of us deserve the chance to make the full pursuit of happiness? To go for the fullness of life? The US Constitution guarantees that every person has the right to the pursuit of happiness. If you have a chance see the movie "Pursuit of Happiness" with Will Smith. After that, you will know deeper what this is...

Well, I have made California home for the last half of my life. For that reason. My pursuit of happiness. They say we may not be able to choose where we are born or who our family is, but some of us can choose where we spend our time, where we choose to make our own pursuit of happiness. California, in its sunny days, blue skies, vastness, complexity, diversity has it all for my one life to call home.

So now, it is my time to give an accounting of what I think the pursuit has in it. What are the great moments and how can we try to incorporate these into our life and time so we may have what some would call the fullest chance at life? All my experiences, including my own, and those of my friends, loved ones, students, and some strangers I have known all add up to what I call the "Four Flashes of Life". I am now writing a book about this to share with a wider audience. It may be a classic paperback book, it may be a "download on demand" I am now not sure. I once told a student group my goal is to be on Oprah, meaning Oprah Winfrey's TV show, that usually guarantees a best-seller. Someone thought I said I want it to be an opera... very cool idea, especially since I know nothing about writing an opera! I want it known that I am open to anything... except that I will not sing this opera! I may be an OK writer, but a singer I am not!

OK... let's get to it. Flash One. It is the *Green Flash*, some may have seen as the sun goes down over the horizon... it is seen by only a few... the last part of the prism of light, as the sun disappears, there is a flash of green... this is really a metaphor for seeking special moments in nature, God's gift to us in the environment of nature...

we do need those moments... crisp air in a winter morning after a fresh snowfall... the whisper of mist from a waterfall on our face... I have seen the green flash once... on the beach in Hawaii... it is a real phenomenon...

Flash Two. The *Pink Flash*. This is romantic love which touches most all of us sooner or later and some of us several times. It is like a whoosh... before you know it, you are so bonded with another in a rush of romance... it can be ageless, unplanned, can end in joy or pain... we all need this to be truly human, and yet we are learning about it all our lives... the lessons go on and get some of us so engrossed and confused, we often think we are starting all over again... yet we must learn from each one and must follow our heart... no easy answers here, just that we cannot avoid this so human part of our full life... when the pink (heart) flash truly hits, you feel like you are in a free fall... its power in life is among the greatest gifts.

Flash Three. The *White Flash*. Whatever a person's faith, there are moments when each of us seems to be spoken to directly or given a clear signal by the Creator. I call these "white moments". Time stands still. There is no worldly explanation. Logic is defied. But an answer is given. A gift seems to be delivered. A messenger shows up. Something unexplainable occurs. Some people spend more time with this, actively pursuing the Creator' guidance. Others deny the Creator, yet admit that they see answers that they cannot trace to a source. Can we pursue answers actively? Can we learn to invoke these powers? A full life seems to include the awareness that we are searching and that this search gets richer and richer as we grow... in the life-long pursuit of happiness, it is hard to avoid some moments that are unexplainable and seem too unreal to be true...

Last flash. The Big *Blue Flash*! This is the moment when one sees one's life purpose. Laying out in front of your feet just like a pathway. Some see it as a picture. Not everyone has this one. Those lucky ones who do describe the moment with excitement. It always takes place with some other loved one present, always takes place in a peaceful place, and people describe that their themes of life come together in a single concept or idea. It can be a company, a career goal, an idea of a central project for one's life... why we seem to justify our existence, education. It seems to occur at mid life, rarely early. People seem to need some pain and confusion and wandering before it is achieved. BUT, those who find it and follow it are the happiest on earth. They seem also to be the bravest, the toughest, and most willing to help others find it. It becomes a passionate pursuit of happiness at the highest level.

With all of these, can we teach them or learn them any faster than what life gives us at its normal pace. Can we get to it faster? My life has taught me there is a natural clock, the Creator's clock, the Greeks called "chiros" (God's time), not "chronos" (Man's time). I had to feel the pain of the search before I saw my own "blue flash". I still look for the green flash now with more passion after I saw the first one in Hawaii. I still seek, though shyly, my Creator's hand in my life... I know it is there, just sometimes it is so hard to see. I still feel the pink flash and it is one of life's biggest mysteries especially when it hits from a 90 degree angle and is unexpected.

My blue flash was the idea of creating CIBU almost 20 years ago. It still is alive, and the sky is blue, more so than ever, I am convinced this is one of everybody's biggest challenges in this world now and in the future. If you can put a life together and put something down here on the planet that did not exist before you... it can be a company, a great product or service, art, music, or a worthwhile pursuit of happiness that is your legacy... if... There could be no greater joy for me than to hope that CIBU is a place and time in people's lives where these great flashes may occur... and that we teach our students to look for these flashes even if they have not seen them yet, because, I will guarantee... they are out there waiting to happen... when you are ready to find them...

Saying Goodbye to Mentors, Saying Hello to New Students

29 September 2009

2009, I said goodbye to two of my dear mentors, Dr. Bill Wolf, Professor Emeritus, Cornell University, and Dr. Dave Feldman, Stanford Ph. D. former Dean of Business at USIU, and our founding Vice President of Academic Affairs here at CIBU. Both died this year and I can still hardly believe that I cannot just simply make a phone call to them to say, "hey, what's on your mind... ?" With a strong cup of coffee, I have been just getting used to saying it... I cannot do that anymore...

These guys were tough! They were tough and yet friendly to me always. They expected my best, even when I had trouble giving it. They never lost faith. They were eternal optimists. They kept working well into their late eighties, my heroes. They lived 24/7 for all of us, took phone calls and rallied into the night. As a young graduate student, I actually thought I was involved in some kind of greater purpose in search of knowledge, somewhat like a young detective in a laboratory with a sense of urgency. Even later, these guys instilled a sense of purpose deeper than most others... it was never sleepy... it was always stand-up-in your chair, like get ready for this...

I suppose that is why I selected them. I mean, I selected these guys to be my beacons. They did not select me, though they would be honored with our association. That is what mentors should be... people we select... by our complete choice... they are somehow tough on us but very compatible with our intellectual soul and spirit...

They speak of mentor-killing. Yes! Actually the phenomenon of people who have to drive away from their guides in life because of various reasons, maybe them, maybe the mentors get too rough.

Be aware of this. But, with these two for me, it was a long life friendship and debate, always, we never agreed totally. That is important to understand. We are not the same mind.

If you have no mentors you are empty of something very powerful and strong. It is up to you to select the mentor, not the other way around... Find what is your hero or heroine in values.

Select him or her. Say hello. Get ready for a big, ride and a farewell someday.

Just another day at the office, I suppose, not for parents, though they would understand and were students too, just for students and ourselves... have a coffee and get ready for the best future you could ever imagine!

So, what is your role in all this? Your unique contribution? Your own gift to the world? You are, after all, a President of that effort, whatever form it will take.

Personal Mission Statement

31 March 2009

I have been taught all my life, from parents to teachers to mentors, that hard work pays off in the end. I followed the advice to this day and yet I understand that there are other forces at work as well... luck, the role of others, and certain golden moments which seem to be accidents, but later appear to be gifts. I have seen highs and lows in the lives of others and in my own. I have seen how fast time can fly and why now at my stage of experience it is important to focus on what is important, where to spend my time and where it could be wasted. Some of the choices are not easy. I perceive an urgency to set forth some statements of personal mission and to get more organized than ever to align my efforts for these critical causes. While I fully intend to go for these goals with unbridled fury, I hope to pay attention, as Buckminster Fuller said, to the stuff which comes in at 90 degree angles... there will be changes and surprises which cause us to adjust, we hope!

The planet has changed lots since I finished my formal education. The world of business is literally a "world business", or maybe the term should be a "planetary economy". There are new problems and new planetary urgencies which now impact b-school education everywhere. The equivalent of natural disasters on the planet in the business education world is a set of man-made problems now deeply embedded in higher education worldwide: overbuilt systems in the US and in other advanced countries; digital technologies which reduce time, effort and possibly scientific rigor; non-symmetrical systems worldwide; vast audiences that are unreachable or unable to afford the cost of education. A colleague in Asia pointed out that only a very small percentage of the total will ever be able to get on airplanes and have a foreign study experience. When a professional discipline or field implodes because of its inability to deal with world forces such as these, it falls from favor, undergoes painful transitions, and may force metamorphosis to a new or lower form of its original good self. Wall Streeters and bankers worldwide are now undergoing this massive shakeout and shakedown. Higher education across the planet may be one of the next big sectors to undergo crises never seen before. I see that my own professional efforts, activities and projects must address the larger planetary economy issues as well as immediate local efforts on a daily basis. It involves me, my leadership, my venue, which is the California International Business University (CIBU), and what I choose to do each day, week, month, and year. This urgency has led me to conclude that my energies must address general causes and some specific career actions which align with my life purpose as a global educator and creator:

Critical Relevance... the urgent need to bring critical relevance, as I know it, to the increasingly irrelevant and jaded world of b-schools so that the customers (students) can get a fair value deal now for the future value of their investment in time, effort, and money.

A Challenging Perspective... the urgent concern for the use and possible abuse of knowledge in the business and financial world... at a time in which the planet is dealing in its larger context with potentially disastrous issues of world hunger, disease, senseless wars, terrorism and out of control natural disasters and economic crises.

Programs, Priorities and Central Projects... As a professional and leader in my chosen field of business school and university level international education, I will devote my time and energy to focused areas which matter and in which I have an actual chance to make a real contribution.

1. I am a global educator... I build bridges... and impact individuals, and that has a multiplier effect

2. I create programs and central projects to effectuate global education

3. I light the fire of the entrepreneurial spirit within each student

4. I must understand deeply the cutting edge of my field to be able to speak credibly as a spokesman-leader, and so I can convey the true value of knowledge to my students

5. I will navigate my chosen institution's (CIBU) impact and growth in its category or ranking, as an institution with correct values for the planetary economy. This will necessarily encompass the positioning of the US and California as central and vital places for the combination of study, research, and application of frontier innovation.

6. I will articulate my message to make sure that hard working, leadership seeking, achievement seeking students can avoid the pitfalls of extreme self interest, elitism, and hubris

7. I will illuminate my students and our student body about the possibility of finding a central life purpose worth everything to pursue, and provide them with my own story and insights about how one might find this...

8. I will challenge the business school community about its collective responsibility for both the proper and improper, harmful uses of financial engineering and other business school influences on our society and the greater global economy.

9. I will challenge my colleagues to do the same.

10. I will challenge my students to lead and foremost to create useful projects, and to help others to do the same.

I reserve the right to update, modify, and enrich this statement in an ongoing way. There is an enormous amount I could write and may in the future to anchor my opinions and positions in empirical data. For example, I have used the words "proper" and "abuse" in this essay, and I realize that much more should follow about what actual values might look like. In essence, this is subjective and everything starts with an opening challenge, and that is exactly what this is... subjective and very personal at heart. Just laying down what you believe and what you stand for and what you intend to do is an incredibly awesome and daunting challenge unto itself. My inspiration for this profound professional step comes from Jeffrey Bennett, Ph. D., the renowned astrophysicist. Dr. Bennett made his own personal mission statement public on his website www.jeffreybennett.com I had never seen anything quite like it. I realized upon reading it that this is a vital step in one's own coming to terms with one's life purpose. I encourage colleagues, students, and friends to consider taking this same step. We create our legacy with concrete actions in moments of utmost clarity and bravery. When you do this, I guarantee it's a step of the toughest and most courageous kind.

Thanks for the Bounty, and Forgive Us for Trying to Understand What We Cannot...

24 November 2009

This was always my favorite holiday. It just seemed like the most "right" and honest one. A time to give thanks and reflect on what our gifts are. More is spent on Christmas and Halloween, but this one just seems like the real one... that brings so many together. And brings us closer to understanding what our life is about.

I am always afraid I will be incomplete on this one... that I will forget something really important to give thanks for... I guess that is just part of being human about Thanksgiving... we cannot bring it all to a neat focus of thanks for all the things and people.

This year there are friends around me who have pain and loss... how can I be thankful, except that they are fighting the good fight on their own to overcome what we all must alone. This year there is joy in my life... some new friends... some new feelings I have not felt for a long time... and there are surprise good gifts... some dear friends who will come to our table to share turkey dinner... one of my best friends who will just show up... a real gift.

And then there are things that I remember that are also gifts of grace but are things given to us which we will never, never understand. One of these mysteries of life I will share on this Thanksgiving. It is a kind of gift, though one that has tragedy written all over it.

We took an adult swim class several summers ago. We got to know Quin. She was one of the swimmers and during the summer she conquered her fear of water and learned to swim so beautifully in the water. She was from a far off Asian land, but had married an American and was living a peaceful productive life at 28, working and finishing her degree at SDSU. At dinner once she told me her goal was to start a company and one day have a big house up on the cliffs in La Jolla overlooking the ocean.

In the horrendous fires that hit San Diego three years ago, Quin and her husband died one night trying to outrun the firestorm. They were found in their car with their dogs they were trying to save.

When we saw the news, it seemed so unreal. But the truth was that the world had lost Quin, and we had lost a friend.

I went through all the stages of grief. The anger, the sense of sadness... then the overwhelming sense of trying to understand or make some sense out of this tragedy. There is no sense to be made. It was just that we had to make peace and go on, not knowing.

I kept up trying to put things together, like somehow I could in an earthly way. No way... I just asked my God to give me some glimpse of it, some hint, something to live with this mystery... why a young, beautiful woman, in her prime, with palpable dreams, would go from us... why?

The gift came one day... after I was just reflecting on everything I knew about Quin... everything we were given to know.

Water. Water is the only thing that can defeat fire. Quin was afraid of water when we first knew her. After a summer of swimming together, you could see how she just sailed along, so unafraid and so free across the water. She had conquered water. Water defeats fire. It is the only thing that can. The circle was complete. Quin had achieved her victory in life over her greatest fear. That gave me so much. Where did it come from? My mind? Where do these things come from? Within us? Or do they come from outside. Are they to be considered small gifts of what we can make sense out of the mystery of life as best we can?

Knowing this all will not bring back Quin, our friend. But, somehow, it helps me get through it better. Just a little bit better. It doesn't help me understand why she was taken so young, or the way it happened. But to know that she conquered something and was so free and happy doing so that beats what took her life away... she made it across that bridge... and seeing her in that water is my gift that goes on, and on. That is a thing that can never be taken away. A connection that gives me some peace.

So Thanksgiving is almost here again, time for friends and good food and deep reflection on our lives. For the easy gifts, and for the ones harder earned. The mystery gifts that we need to get through. This one is for Quin... thanks for the sight of you skimming so gracefully across the water with such joy. You will take that to the stars. I will take that picture of you with me for as long as I can. Happy Thanksgiving. Thanksgiving... the time to ponder what we are, what we have and the only very small hints at the mysteries of the universe.

Five

Epilogue

December 30, 2009

May Old Acquaintances Be Forgot...
but They Cannot Be Forgotten...

Something happened in July 2009 and ended, at least for now, in late December, 2009. During these months, I wrote and wrote, and what you have read here is what I produced. My shared concerns and thoughts about our business school world and the human issues which present every day. It was, during these months, like my life was filled with the sound of music... something wonderful happened, by accident, came in on one of those 90 degree angles that Buckminster Fuller talks about.

It was like a wind at my back, when I used to skate on lakes. It was like a wind under my wings to write, to stay up late and put down my thoughts for others. That "wind" was a creative force that made me feel like writing. I guess the artist feels the same escape when he or she goes to canvas to paint in passion...

It was a good time to write about things in 2009. Lots was happening. There was lots to write about. Wall Street had almost crashed, and Main Street was bleeding. We who lead business schools needed to speak out and challenge each other.

Some amazing things happened with our business school, the California International Business University (CIBU) during this period. We grew and encountered some of the most human issues we ever faced. There were losses of dear ones, there were new additions, new places, new faces, and some serendipity that confounded us. I tried to capture some of the agony and ecstasy in these moments in these essays.

During this time, I discovered I needed to set forth my own personal mission statement. Dr. Jeffrey Bennett, came into our community and provided inspiration to do this. We were challenged. We rose to this challenge. My own first attempt at a life purpose statement is contained in these essays. Others are still working on theirs.

I lost two mentors this year. It gave me the chance to reflect and write about what mentors really are and what they should be. It was not easy.

I never met some of the heroes I wrote about. The war widow. The Wall Street mavericks who are working against the creeping "gaming of America" by the clever Wall Street brains who would run off with our assets. I never expect to see these people, but I know they are out there in our larger family of friends.

There are moments in the lives of all of us, I am convinced, that are crossroads... choices to go away or to stay, choices to run or to stand and fight... choices to love or let go... or to love and let go, maybe one of the toughest.

We never know what our choices will bring, and we do still make mistakes... big ones. Just about when we may think we get the cultural context, understand the cultural differences, we are reminded by events that we were 180 degrees off from how we were actually received by those we wanted to have as friends. We are forever students, even though some of us are put in the role of "teacher", we must learn what we missed and hope we do not miss it again.

But we do learn that when we run away, nothing good ever happens.. We must face our problems, even when there is pain. Somehow, we live on faith that better days will come.

That brings me full circle. I loved those days and especially late nights when I just had to write. I loved the sound of music in my inner world when I was sharing and pouring forth. The next book on life's four great flashes is coming and will be roaring forward when it starts...

I guess I am convinced that one of the strongest gifts we are given are those who we love and who love us. Friends and friendship. It is the true Ship of Friends that sails on forever...

This book will go out to the world through the magic of e-publishing... it will be available to the world, have an ISBN number and even find its way to the Library of Congress. It will be read by people who do not even know me or the people I write about. Some of the essays have already been seen by strangers around the world who now are friends. Yet if it touches just a few lives to make more of their friendships and understand who their truest friends are, that is the "biggest" audience I could hope for... I am proud of the openness I was able to muster. I deeply treasure the people whose lives touched mine during this past year. I cherish the source of this inspiration and need it in my life again. Some of the best friends in my life were actors in this drama... some are still here with me, some have left. I still have hope that none were truly lost.

But my purpose was accomplished, here in these pages, however I got it done... the young presidents of the global business world... their lives and loves were touched... they are the ones who this was for. My job, after all, and my purpose, is to be the Father Lion of my pride, to watch for predators, to protect my community, to set the strong, fast example. But, this is the moment in time that I am the Lion in winter... it is a tough season at the end of this year... but the Father Lion in me needs to bring his strength and be human and go onward and upward...

I need the sound of music in the late nights when I write... it is the wind at my back, beneath my wings... Old acquaintances will not be forgot... they can never be forgotten. They were not meant to be lost. They were meant to be our friends forever. True friends can never be lost. Happy New Year. Cherish what you do have, and never believe that a true friend has been lost...